BinaryCoder X

Web development essentials

"Dedicated to the curious minds and relentless dreamers—the ones who see beyond the lines of code and envision digital landscapes yet to be explored. May 'Web Development Essentials' be a guiding light in your journey, sparking inspiration and empowering you to weave the future of the web with passion and innovation. This book is for you, the architects of the digital frontier. Happy coding!"

"In the realm of pixels and possibilities, 'Web Development Essentials' is not just a guide; it's a symphony of code, an invitation to dance with the languages that shape the digital canvas. Let BinaryCoder X be your maestro, guiding you through the artistry, the innovation, and the relentless pursuit of excellence in the world of web development. Unleash your creativity, for every keystroke has the potential to redefine the online experience. Happy coding!"

BinaryCoder X

Contents

1.

2.

3.

4.

5.

6.

7.

8.

9.

10.

11.

12.

13.

14.

15.

16.

17.

18.

19.

20.

21.

22.

Foreword

Foreword

In the ever-evolving landscape of the digital frontier, the ability to craft captivating web experiences is both an art and a science. "Web Development Essentials" by BinaryCoder X is not just a guide; it's an invitation to embark on a transformative journey into the heart of web development.

BinaryCoder X, a seasoned navigator in the realm of binary possibilities, brings forth a treasure trove of insights and wisdom in this comprehensive exploration of the essentials. This isn't merely a compilation of technical details; it's a testament to the passion and dedication required to master the craft of web development.

As you delve into the pages of this book, be prepared to traverse the foundational elements—from the keystrokes of HTML, the stylistic symphony of CSS, to the dynamic dance orchestrated by JavaScript. BinaryCoder X demystifies the complexities, making these languages not just tools but instruments to compose digital symphonies.

But this journey goes beyond syntax. It's a holistic exploration of the principles that shape the digital landscape. BinaryCoder X shares the significance of version control in collaborative coding, unveils the power of APIs in connecting digital ecosystems, and unravels the secrets of performance optimization to create lightning-fast web experiences.

"Web Development Essentials" is a compass pointing towards best practices, innovative strategies, and the continuous pursuit of knowledge. BinaryCoder X doesn't just teach; it ignites a spark of curiosity, encouraging you to explore, experiment, and evolve.

Whether you're a novice on the coding horizon or a seasoned developer navigating through the digital currents, let this book be your companion. BinaryCoder X extends an open invitation to discover the artistry, the innovation, and the relentless pursuit of excellence that defines the world of web development.

So, dear reader, prepare to be captivated, inspired, and equipped with the essentials that will empower you on your web development odyssey. BinaryCoder X welcomes you to a world where every line of code tells a story, and every webpage is an opportunity to create something extraordinary. Happy coding!

Preface

Welcome to "Web Development Essentials" by BinaryCoder X, a journey into the core elements that empower the digital world. In this dynamic realm of zeros and ones, where innovation meets functionality, BinaryCoder X serves as your guide through the intricacies of web development.

This book is not just a compilation of technical details; it's a narrative that unfolds the secrets behind creating immersive and responsive web experiences. BinaryCoder X takes you beyond the syntax and into the artistry of coding, unraveling the threads that weave HTML, CSS, and JavaScript into the vibrant tapestry of the internet.

From the foundational HTML shaping the structure to the cascading styles of CSS bringing life to design, and the dynamic dance of JavaScript adding interactivity – BinaryCoder X demystifies these essentials. But this isn't just about the languages; it's about understanding the architecture, mastering the tools, and embracing the principles that transform lines of code into digital masterpieces.

Each chapter is a portal into the multifaceted world of web development, exploring not only the technical intricacies but also the best practices, the innovative strategies, and the art of continuous learning. BinaryCoder X invites you to navigate the terrain of version control, dive into the realm of APIs, and ascend to the peaks of performance optimization.

Whether you are a budding developer or a seasoned coder, "Web Development Essentials" is designed to be your compass, helping you navigate the ever-changing landscape of web technologies. It's not just a manual; it's a conversation with BinaryCoder X, an experienced navigator in the binary seas, ready to share insights, strategies, and a passion for crafting the digital future.

So, buckle up for an enlightening journey. Let "Web Development Essentials" be your companion as you embark on the thrilling adventure of building the web. BinaryCoder X welcomes you to a world where every line of code is a brushstroke, and every webpage is a canvas waiting to be brought   to   life.

Acknowledgement

Acknowledgments

In the symphony of coding, no masterpiece is created alone. "Web Development Essentials" is a testament to the collaborative spirit that defines the world of web development. As I pen down these acknowledgments, my heart brims with gratitude for those whose support, expertise, and inspiration have shaped this journey.

First and foremost, my appreciation goes to the vibrant community of developers, learners, and creators. Your passion fuels the ever-evolving landscape of web technologies. It's your enthusiasm that breathes life into the digital realm.

To the mentors and educators who illuminate the path of knowledge, thank you for sharing your wisdom and guiding the next generation of developers. Your dedication is the lighthouse that helps us navigate through the complexities of coding.

A special nod to the tireless contributors in the open-source community. Your commitment to collaboration and shared learning is the backbone of innovation. Together, we build the future of the web, one commit at a time.

To the pioneers in web development, whose groundbreaking work laid the foundation for this book—your trailblazing efforts continue to inspire and shape the way we code and create.

A heartfelt thank you to the editors, designers, and everyone behind the scenes who transformed words into a visual and tactile experience. Your dedication to detail and creativity brought this project to life.

I extend my gratitude to family and friends whose unwavering support sustained me throughout this journey. Your encouragement fueled late-night coding sessions and fueled the determination to turn concepts into chapters.

Last but certainly not least, to you, dear reader. Your curiosity and thirst for knowledge drive the essence of this book. May these pages empower you on your web development odyssey and inspire the creation of digital wonders.

In the spirit of collaboration and shared learning, let's continue to push the boundaries of what's possible in the ever-expanding universe of web development.

8

Happy coding!

BinaryCoder   X

1

HTML, or Hypertext Markup Language

HTML, or Hypertext Markup Language, is the standard markup language used to structure content on the web. It utilizes a system of tags to define elements such as headings, paragraphs, links, images, and more. These tags provide a hierarchical structure, allowing browsers to render and display content accurately. HTML forms the backbone of web pages, acting as the foundational structure upon which Cascading Style Sheets (CSS) and JavaScript can be applied to enhance presentation and interactivity.

2

CSS, or Cascading Style Sheets

CSS, or Cascading Style Sheets, is a styling language used in web development to control the presentation and layout of HTML documents. It allows developers to apply styles such as colors, fonts, spacing, and positioning to HTML elements. By separating the structure (HTML) from the presentation (CSS), it enables consistency, reusability, and easier maintenance of web pages. CSS operates on a "cascading" principle, where styles can be inherited or overridden, providing flexibility in design while ensuring a cohesive visual experience across a website.

3

JavaScript

JavaScript is a programming language that enables dynamic and interactive behavior on web pages. It runs in web browsers and allows developers to manipulate the content, structure, and styling of HTML documents in real-time. JavaScript is commonly used to create features like form validation, image sliders, and responsive interfaces. It plays a crucial role in client-side scripting, enabling user interactions without requiring page reloads. Additionally, with the advent of server-side JavaScript (Node.js), it can be used for backend development as well.

4

Responsive Design

Responsive Design refers to the approach of designing websites to provide an optimal viewing and interaction experience across a variety of devices and screen sizes. This is achieved by using flexible grids and layouts, along with media queries in CSS, to adapt the presentation of content based on the device characteristics. Responsive design ensures that websites look and function well on desktops, laptops, tablets, and smartphones, contributing to a seamless user experience regardless of the device being used.

5

Version Control

Version Control, exemplified by tools like Git, is a system that tracks changes in code, allowing collaboration among developers and facilitating project management. It maintains a history of modifications, enabling teams to work on different aspects of a project concurrently. Version control helps avoid conflicts, rollback to previous states, and merge changes effectively. Git, in particular, is widely used for its distributed nature, branching capabilities, and compatibility with platforms like GitHub, GitLab, and Bitbucket, fostering collaborative and organized software development.

6

A Text Editor or Integrated Development Environment (IDE)

A Text Editor or Integrated Development Environment (IDE) serves as a software tool for writing and editing code. Examples include Visual Studio Code and Atom. These tools provide features like syntax highlighting, auto-completion, and debugging support, enhancing the coding experience. Text editors are lightweight and customizable, while IDEs often include additional features such as built-in terminals, version control integration, and project management tools, catering to the specific needs and preferences of developers.

7

Browser Developer Tools

Browser Developer Tools are built-in functionalities within web browsers that assist developers in debugging, optimizing, and inspecting web pages. These tools provide a range of features, including live editing of HTML, CSS, and JavaScript, network monitoring, and console for logging errors and messages. Developers use these tools to diagnose issues, analyze performance, and test changes in real-time, contributing to the development and refinement of web applications.

8

Command Line Basics

Command Line Basics involve familiarity with using a command-line interface (CLI) to interact with a computer's operating system. This includes tasks such as navigating directories, copying or moving files, and executing commands. Understanding the command line is crucial for efficient file management, running scripts, and using various development tools. Proficiency in the command line enhances a developer's ability to perform tasks more quickly and precisely, contributing to a smoother development workflow.

9

Web Hosting Basics

Web Hosting Basics involve understanding how to deploy a website on a server and manage its accessibility on the internet. This includes concepts like domain registration, configuring DNS settings, and selecting a hosting provider. Developers need to grasp the fundamentals of server environments, file transfer protocols (e.g., FTP), and security considerations for hosting web applications. A solid understanding of web hosting ensures that websites are accessible, secure, and performant for users worldwide.

10

Basic SEO Principles

Basic SEO Principles refer to foundational concepts in Search Engine Optimization. This involves optimizing web content to improve its visibility and ranking on search engine results pages (SERPs). Key principles include using relevant keywords, creating descriptive and concise meta tags, having well-structured URLs, and ensuring mobile responsiveness. Understanding SEO helps developers and content creators make websites more discoverable to search engines, ultimately attracting organic traffic and improving the overall online presence of a website.

11

HTTP/HTTPS Protocols

HTTP/HTTPS Protocols are fundamental to web communication. HTTP (Hypertext Transfer Protocol) and its secure version, HTTPS, define how data is transmitted between a user's web browser and a website's server. HTTPS encrypts data for secure communication, crucial for protecting sensitive information such as login credentials and payment details. Developers must understand these protocols to ensure data integrity, security, and proper functioning of web applications.

12

AJAX (Asynchronous JavaScript and XML)

AJAX (Asynchronous JavaScript and XML) is a technique in web development that allows asynchronous communication between a web browser and a web server. It enables the updating of parts of a web page without requiring a full page reload. AJAX is commonly implemented using JavaScript to send and receive data in the background, enhancing the user experience by providing dynamic and responsive content. This technology is crucial for creating interactive and seamless web applications.

13

Web APIs (Application Programming Interfaces)

Web APIs (Application Programming Interfaces) enable interaction between different software systems over the web. In web development, APIs facilitate communication between a web application and external services or data sources. Developers use APIs to retrieve data, send information, or perform specific actions, enhancing the functionality of their applications. Understanding how to integrate and work with APIs is essential for building dynamic and feature-rich web applications that can leverage external resources.

14

Build Tools, such as npm and webpack

Build Tools, such as npm and webpack, are integral to modern web development workflows. They automate tasks like bundling, minification, and transpilation of code, streamlining the process of preparing code for production. Build tools help manage dependencies, optimize assets, and enhance performance. By incorporating these tools into development pipelines, developers can ensure efficient and consistent build processes, ultimately leading to well-organized and optimized web applications.

15

Package Managers

Package Managers, like npm (Node Package Manager) and yarn, simplify the management of project dependencies. These tools automate the installation, updating, and removal of libraries and packages used in a web development project. Package managers help maintain a consistent and reproducible environment across different development environments, ensuring that collaborators work with the same set of dependencies and versions. This contributes to smoother collaboration and more reliable development processes.

16

Basic Understanding of Databases

Basic Understanding of Databases is essential for web developers. It involves knowledge of how to interact with databases to store, retrieve, update, and delete data. Common database systems include MySQL, PostgreSQL, and MongoDB. Developers need to understand database design, normalization, and the use of SQL (Structured Query Language) or NoSQL queries. This knowledge is crucial for building dynamic and data-driven web applications where persistent storage and retrieval of information are integral components.

17

Security Best Practices

Security Best Practices are critical for protecting web applications against vulnerabilities and unauthorized access. Developers need to implement measures such as input validation, secure authentication, and encryption of sensitive data. They should be aware of common security threats like SQL injection, Cross-Site Scripting (XSS), and Cross-Site Request Forgery (CSRF) to prevent potential exploits. Regular security audits, staying informed about the latest security trends, and adhering to best practices contribute to building robust and secure web applications.

18

Browser Compatibility

Browser Compatibility is the consideration of ensuring that web applications work consistently across different web browsers. Developers need to test and optimize their code for compatibility with popular browsers such as Chrome, Firefox, Safari, and Edge. This involves addressing variations in rendering engines, CSS support, and JavaScript implementations. Ensuring cross-browser compatibility enhances the user experience, reaching a broader audience and preventing potential issues that may arise from differences in browser behavior.

19

Performance Optimization

Performance Optimization is the practice of enhancing the speed and efficiency of web applications. Developers employ various techniques, including optimizing images, minimizing HTTP requests, leveraging browser caching, and using content delivery networks (CDNs). Efficient coding practices, such as lazy loading and code splitting, contribute to faster page load times. Performance optimization is crucial for providing a smooth and responsive user experience, reducing bounce rates, and improving a website's overall ranking in search engines.

20

Continuous Learning

Continuous Learning is an ongoing essential for web developers. Given the dynamic nature of web technologies, staying updated with the latest frameworks, tools, and best practices is crucial. Following industry blogs, participating in developer communities, attending conferences, and exploring new technologies contribute to professional growth. Continuous learning ensures developers are well-equipped to adapt to evolving trends, tackle challenges, and deliver high-quality, modern web applications.